Husband

A BOOK FOR MY Husband

PAMELA WINTERBOURNE

WELLERAN POLTARNEES

LAUGHING ELEPHANT   MMIII

COPYRIGHT © 2003 BLUE LANTERN STUDIO

ISBN 1-883211-77-8

FIRST PRINTING   ALL RIGHTS RESERVED   PRINTED IN CHINA

LAUGHING ELEPHANT BOOKS
3645 INTERLAKE AVENUE NORTH   SEATTLE   98103

www.LAUGHINGELEPHANT.com

I thank you for being my husband,

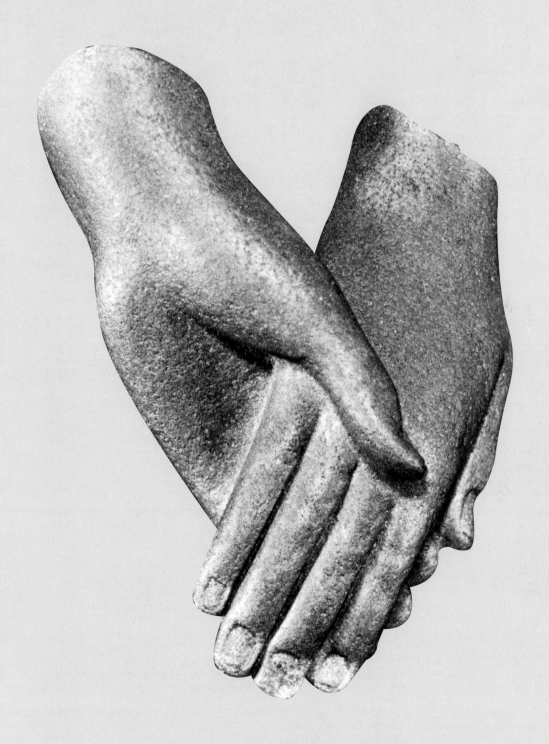

and I offer this book
as a reflection of my gratitude.

I am glad that you admired me,
for that was the beginning.

Your romantic impulses
surprised and delighted me.

You found that you needed me,
and I found that I needed you.

Thank you for giving me flowers,

and many thoughtful gifts.

11

Haskell Coffin

We have always been able to
laugh together.

13

I am honored that you have
shared your deepest thoughts,

and have always cared about
my thoughts and feelings.

Your patience has been seen
and appreciated.

I will always remember
the many adventures
we have had together.

Thank you for your trust.

I enjoy our
everyday companionship.

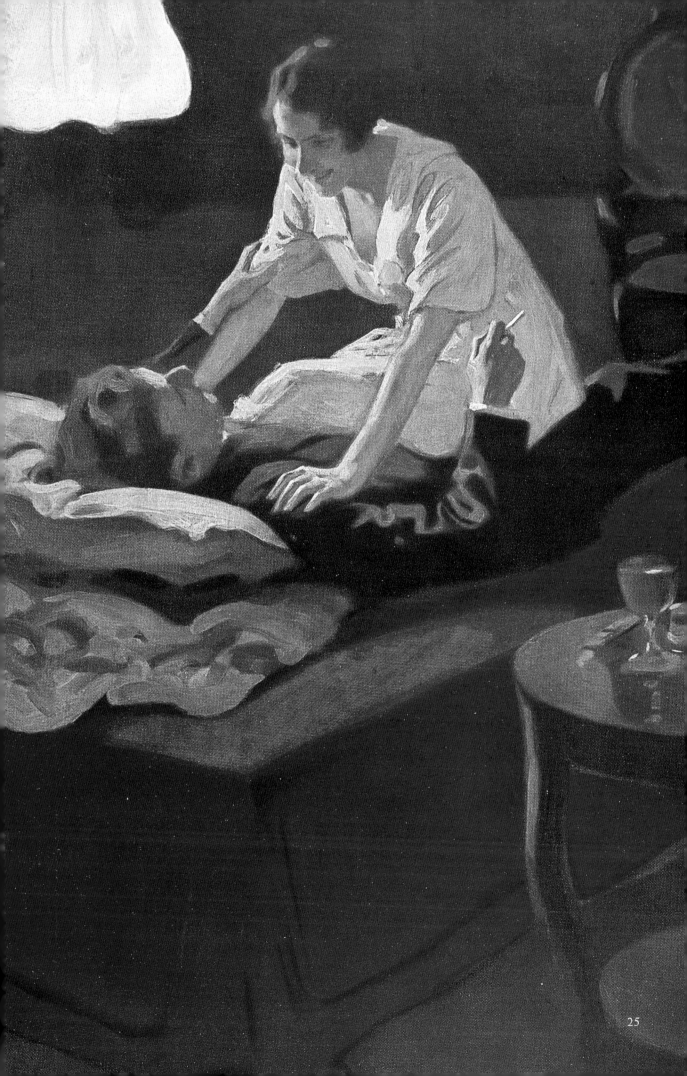

We have certainly had
differences and tense moments,
but we have surmounted them.

Most of all I thank you
for your love,

and your willingness
to tell me of that love.

Picture Credits

Cover	McClelland Barclay. Magazine cover, 1929.
Half Title	Unknown. Magazine illustration, n.d.
Frontis	Henri Le Sidaner. "Table dans la Verdure," 1926.
Title Page	Unknown. French postcard, n.d.
Copyright	W.T. Benda. Magazine illustration, 1921.
ix	Felix Vallotton. "Private Conversation," 1898.
1	Fragment of 18th dynasty Egyptian statue.
2	Unknown. Advertising illustration, n.d.
3	Unknown. Advertising illustration, 1934.
4	Henry Salem Hubbell. "Susanna," 1915.
5	McClelland Barclay. Magazine cover, 1932.
6	Thomas Webb. Magazine illustration, n.d.
7	Howard Pyle. From The Island of Enchantment, 1905.
8	B. Wennerberg. "Morgengabe," c. 1920.
9	Neysa McMein. Magazine cover, 1928.
10	William McGregor Paxton. "The Blue Jar," 1913.
11	Haskell Coffin. Magazine cover, 1930.
12	John La Gatta. Magazine illustration, 1934.
13	Lynn Buckham. Magazine illustration, 1955.
14	Unknown. Advertising illustration, 1932.
15	Tom Lovell. Magazine illustration, 1949.
16/17	John La Gatta. Magazine illustration, 1936.
18	Edmundson. Magazine cover, 1932.
19	Coles Phillips. From A Young Man's Fancy, 1912.
20	Unknown. Advertising illustration, n.d.
21	McClelland Barclay. Magazine cover, 1940.
22	Unknown. Advertising illustration, 1927.
23	Lester Ralph. Magazine cover, 1915.
24	Robert Patterson. "Couple Poolside," c. 1950.
25	B. Wennerberg. "Süfse Last," c. 1920.
26	Austin Briggs. Advertising illustration, n.d.
27	Coby Whitmore. Magazine illustration, n.d.
28	Coby Whitmore. Magazine illustration, 1951.
29	Unknown. Magazine cover, 1937.
30	Unknown. Advertising illustration, 1928.
31	Unknown. Magazine cover, 1936.
34	Rockwell Kent. From This Is My Own, 1940.
Back Cover	Unknown. Advertising illustration, c. 1941.

Colophon

Designed at Blue Lantern Studio by Mike Harrison and Sacheverell Darling

Typeset in Weiss and Didot